Piano - Vocal - Guitar

THE GREAT BIG BOOK OF CHILDREN'S SONGS

ISBN 0-7935-3918-8

HAL•LEONARD™
CORPORATION

7777 W. BLUEMOUND RD. P.O. BOX 13819 MILWAUKEE, WI 53213

A-HUNTING WE WILL GO

Traditional

ARE YOU SLEEPING

Traditional

Frè - re Jac - ques, Frè - re Jac - ques,
Are you sleep - ing, are you sleep - ing,

Dor - mez vous, dor - mez vous? Son - nez les ma - ti - nes,
Broth - er John, Broth - er John? Morn - ing bells are ring - ing,

Repeat ad lib.

son - nez les ma - ti - nes, Din din don, din din don.
morn - ing bells are ring - ing, Ding ding ding dong, ding ding ding dong.

ABC-DEF-GHI

Words by JOE RAPOSO and JON STONE
Music by JOE RAPOSO

THE BALLAD OF DAVY CROCKETT

from Walt Disney's DAVY CROCKETT: KING OF THE WILD FRONTIER

Words by TOM BLACKBURN
Music by GEORGE BRUNS

VERSES

4.

Andy Jackson is our gen'ral's name,
His reg'lar soldiers we'll put to shame,
Them redskin varmints us Volunteers'll tame,
'Cause we got the guns with the sure-fire aim.
Davy — Davy Crockett,
The champion of us all!

5.

Headed back to war from the ol' home place,
But Red Stick was leadin' a merry chase,
Fightin' an' burnin' at a devil's pace
South to the swamps on the Florida Trace.
Davy — Davy Crockett,
Trackin' the redskins down!

6.

Fought single-handed through the Injun War
Till the Creeks was whipped an' peace was in store,
An' while he was handlin' this risky chore,
Made hisself a legend for evermore.
Davy — Davy Crockett,
King of the wild frontier!

7.

He give his word an' he give his hand
That his Injun friends could keep their land,
An' the rest of his life he took the stand
That justice was due every redskin band.
Davy — Davy Crockett,
Holdin' his promise dear!

8.

Home fer the winter with his family,
Happy as squirrels in the ol' gum tree,
Bein' the father he wanted to be,
Close to his boys as the pod an' the pea.
Davy — Davy Crockett,
Holdin' his young 'uns dear!

9.

But the ice went out an' the warm winds came
An' the meltin' snow showed tracks of game,
An' the flowers of Spring filled the woods with flame,
An' all of a sudden life got too tame.
Davy — Davy Crockett,
Headin' on West again!

10.

Off through the woods we're ridin' along,
Makin' up yarns an' singin' a song,
He's ringy as a b'ar an' twict as strong,
An' knows he's right 'cause he ain't often wrong.
Davy — Davy Crockett,
The man who don't know fear!

11.

Lookin' fer a place where the air smells clean,
Where the trees is tall an' the grass is green,
Where the fish is fat in an untouched stream,
An' the teemin' woods is a hunter's dream.
Davy — Davy Crockett,
Lookin' fer Paradise!

12.

Now he'd lost his love an' his grief was gall,
In his heart he wanted to leave it all,
An' lose himself in the forests tall,
But he answered instead his country's call.
Davy — Davy Crockett,
Beginnin' his campaign!

13.

Needin' his help they didn't vote blind,
They put in Davy 'cause he was their kind,
Sent up to Nashville the best they could find,
A fightin' spirit an' a thinkin' mind.
Davy — Davy Crockett,
Choice of the whole frontier!

14.

The votes were counted an' he won hands down,
So they sent him off to Washin'ton town
With his best dress suit still his buckskins brown,
A livin' legend of growin' renown.
Davy — Davy Crockett,
The Canebrake Congressman!

15.

He went off to Congress an' served a spell,
Fixin' up the Gover'ment an' laws as well,
Took over Washin'ton so we heered tell
An' patched up the crack in the Liberty Bell.
Davy — Davy Crockett,
Seein' his duty clear!

16.

Him an' his jokes travelled all through the land,
An' his speeches made him friends to beat the band,
His politickin' was their favorite brand
An' everyone wanted to shake his hand.
Davy — Davy Crockett,
Helpin' his legend grow!

17.

He knew when he spoke he sounded the knell
Of his hopes for White House an' fame as well,
But he spoke out strong so hist'ry books tell
An patched up the crack in the Liberty Bell.
Davy — Davy Crockett,
Seein' his duty clear!

BEAUTY AND THE BEAST

from Walt Disney's BEAUTY AND THE BEAST

Lyrics by HOWARD ASHMAN
Music by ALAN MENKEN

Tale as old as time, song as old as rhyme. Beau - ty and the Beast.

THE BARE NECESSITIES

from Walt Disney's THE JUNGLE BOOK

Words and Music by
TERRY GILKYSON

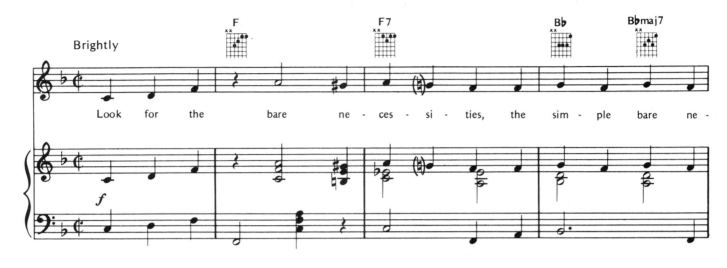

Look for the bare ne - ces - si - ties, the sim - ple bare ne -

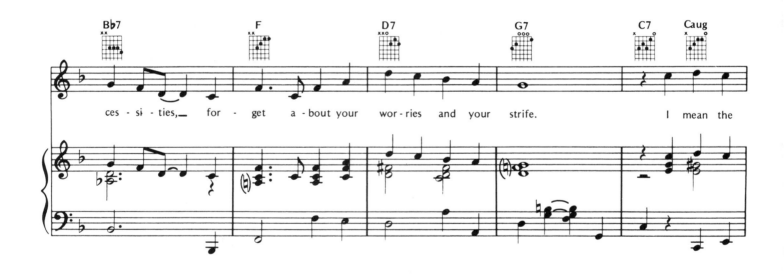

ces - si - ties,__ for - get a - bout your wor - ries and your strife. I mean the

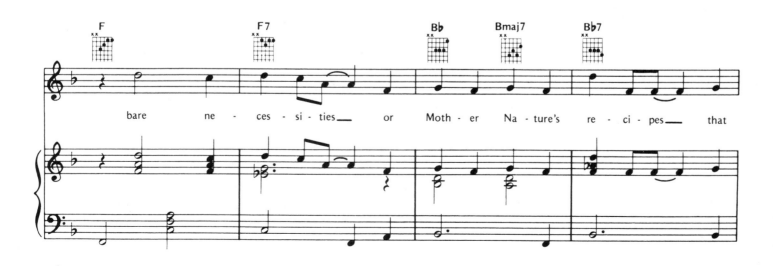

bare ne - ces - si - ties__ or Moth - er Na - ture's re - ci - pes__ that

BE KIND TO YOUR PARENTS

from FANNY

Words and Music by
HAROLD ROME

BEIN' GREEN

Words and Music by
JOE RAPOSO

A BICYCLE BUILT FOR TWO
(a/k/a DAISY BELL)

Words and Music by
HARRY DACRE

THE BIBLE TELLS ME SO

Words and Music by
DALE EVANS

THE BRADY BUNCH
Theme from the Paramount Television Series THE BRADY BUNCH

Words and Music by SHERWOOD SCHWARTZ
and FRANK DEVOL

BUFFALO GALS
(Won't You Come Out Tonight?)

Words and Music by
COOL WHITE (JOHN HODGES)

Buf-fa-lo gals, won't ya come out to-night, won't ya
Yes, pret-ty boys, we'll come out to-night, we'll

come out to-night, won't ya come out to-night? Buf-fa-lo gals, won't ya
come out to-night, we'll come out to-night. Yes, pret-ty boys, we'll

come out to-night and dance by the light of the moon?
come out to-night and dance by the light of the moon.

"C" IS FOR COOKIE

Now, what starts with the letter C?

Words and Music by
JOE RAPOSO

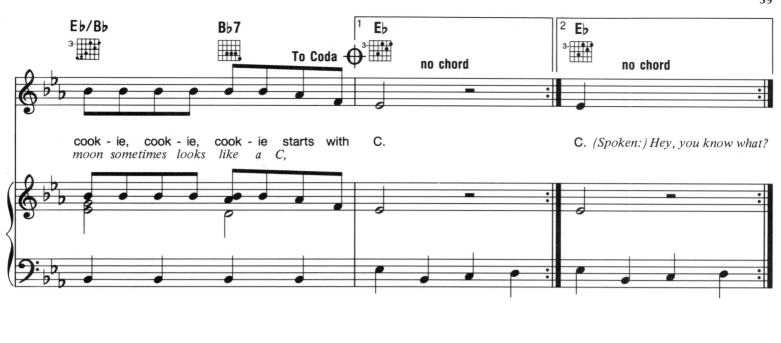

cook - ie, cook - ie, cook - ie starts with C.

moon sometimes looks like a C,

C. *(Spoken:) Hey, you know what?*

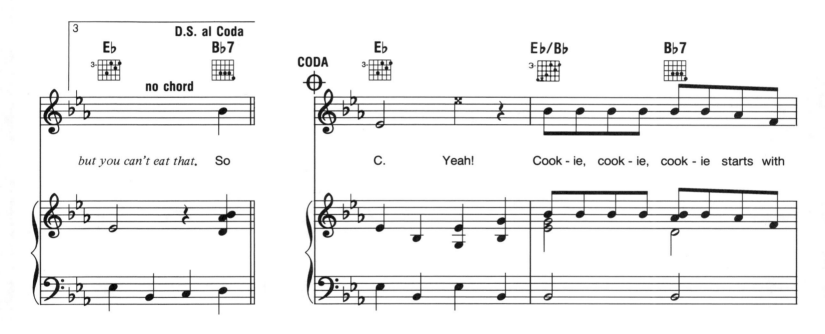

but you can't eat that. So

C. Yeah! Cook - ie, cook - ie, cook - ie starts with

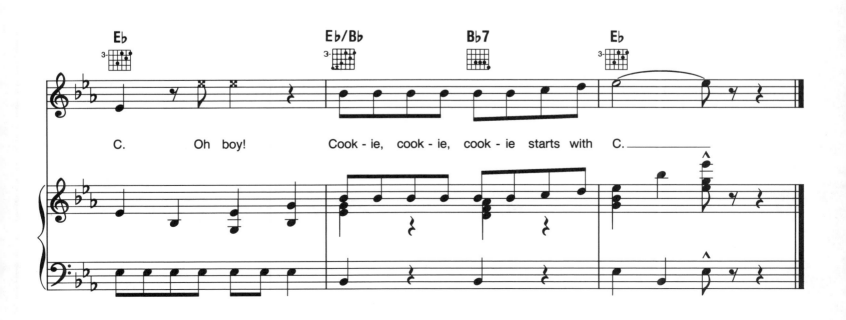

C. Oh boy! Cook - ie, cook - ie, cook - ie starts with C.

THE CANDY MAN

from WILLY WONKA AND THE CHOCOLATE FACTORY

Words and Music by LESLIE BRICUSSE
and ANTHONY NEWLEY

CASPER THE FRIENDLY GHOST

from the Paramount Cartoon

Words by MACK DAVID
Music by JERRY LIVINGSTON

CIRCLE OF LIFE
from Walt Disney Pictures' THE LION KING

Music by ELTON JOHN
Lyrics by TIM RICE

Same tempo, gently rhythmic

(African chant continues)

THE CRAWDAD SONG

Traditional

With a lively beat, in 2

1. You get a line and I'll get a pole, my

2.-5. *See additional lyrics*

hon - ey. You get a line and

I'll get a pole, oh, babe.

Additional Lyrics

2. Get up old man, you slept too late, honey, (twice)
Get up old man, you slept too late,
Last piece of crawdad's on your plate,
Honey, sugar baby mine.

3. Get up old woman, you slept too late, honey, (twice)
Get up old woman, you slept too late, honey,
Crawdad man done passed your gate,
Honey, sugar baby mine.

4. What you gonna do when the lake goes dry, (twice)
What you gonna do when the lake goes dry,
Sit on the bank and watch the crawdads die,
Honey, sugar baby mine.

5. What you gonna do when the crawdads die, honey? (twice)
What you gonna do when the crawdads die,
Sit on the bank until I cry,
Honey, sugar baby mine.

CRUELLA de VIL
from Walt Disney's 101 DALMATIONS

Words and Music by
MEL LEVEN

Cru - el - la De Ville,___ Cru - el - la De Ville,___ If she does-n't scare___ you no ev - il thing will.___ To see her is to take a sud - den chill.___ Cur-

DID YOU EVER SEE A LASSIE?

Anonymous

FEED THE BIRDS

from Walt Disney's MARY POPPINS

Words and Music by RICHARD M. SHERMAN
and ROBERT B. SHERMAN

62

DITES-MOI
(TELL ME WHY)
from SOUTH PACIFIC

Lyrics by OSCAR HAMMERSTEIN II
Music by RICHARD RODGERS

Moderato e semplice

Di - tes - moi _____ Pour - quoi _____
Tell me why _____ The sky _____

La vie est bel - le, Di - tes - moi _____ Pour - quoi _____
is filled with mu - sic, Tell me why _____ We fly _____

763-2

DOWN BY THE STATION

Traditional

Down by the sta - tion ear - ly in the morn - ing, see the lit - tle puf - fer - bil - lies all in a

EDELWEISS
from THE SOUND OF MUSIC

Lyrics by OSCAR HAMMERSTEIN II
Music by RICHARD RODGERS

EVERYTHING IS BEAUTIFUL

Words and Music by
RAY STEVENS

2. We shouldn't care about the length of his hair or the color of his skin,
   Don't worry about what shows from without but the love that lives within,
   We gonna get it all together now and everything gonna work out fine,
   Just take a little time to look on the good side my friend and straighten it out in your mind.

(MEET)
THE FLINTSTONES
from THE FLINTSTONES

Words and Music by W. HANNA,
J. BARBERA and H. CURTIN

FROG WENT A-COURTIN'

Anonymous

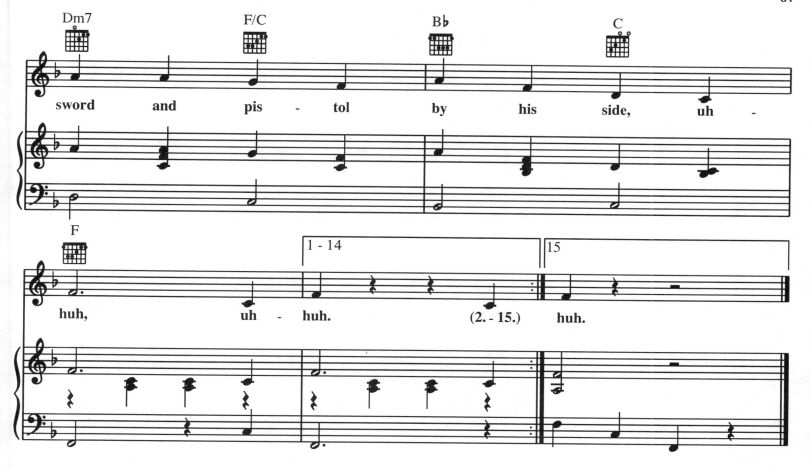

Additional Lyrics

2. Well, he rode down to Miss Mouses's door, uh-huh, uh-huh.
   Well, he rode down to Miss Mouses's door,
   Where he had often been before, uh-huh, uh-huh.

3. He took Miss Mousie on his knee, uh-huh, uh-huh.
   He took Miss Mousie on his knee,
   Said, "Miss Mousie will you marry me?" Uh-huh, uh-huh.

4. "I'll have to ask my Uncle Rat, etc.
   See what he will say to that." etc.

5. "Without my Uncle Rat's consent,
   I would not marry the President."

6. Well, Uncle Rat laughed and shook his fat sides,
   To think his niece would be a bride.

7. Well, Uncle Rat rode off to town
   To buy his niece a wedding gown.

8. "Where will the wedding supper be?"
   "Way down yonder in a hollow tree."

9. "What will wedding supper be?"
   "A fried mosquito and a roasted flea."

10. First to come in were two little ants,
    Fixing around to have a dance.

11. Next to come in was a bumble bee,
    Bouncing a fiddle on his knee.

12. Next to come in was a fat sassy lad,
    Thinks himself as big as his dad.

13. Thinks himself a man indeed,
    Because he chews the tobacco weed.

14. And next to come in was a big tomcat,
    He swallowed the frog and the mouse and the rat.

15. Next to come in was a big old snake,
    He chased the party into the lake.

GETTING TO KNOW YOU

from THE KING AND I

Words by OSCAR HAMMERSTEIN II
Music by RICHARD RODGERS

GO IN AND OUT THE WINDOW

Traditional

GO TELL AUNT RHODY

Traditional

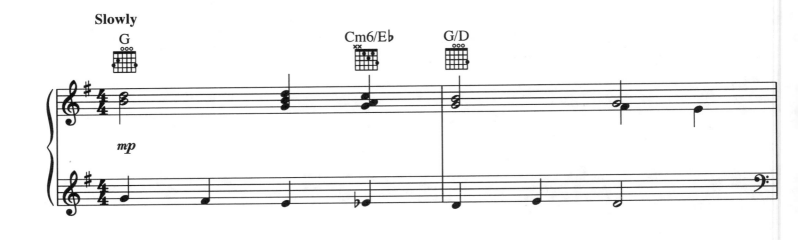

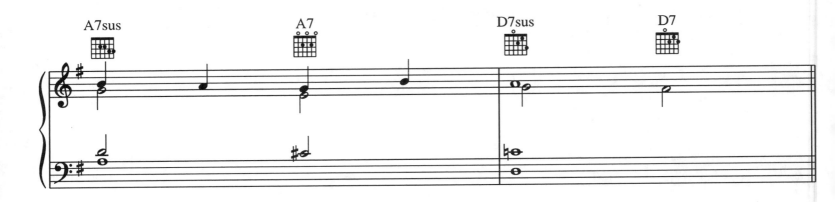

1. Go tell Aunt Rho - dy,

2.-5. *(See additional lyrics)*

Additional Lyrics

2. The one she was saving, *(three times)*
   To make a feather bed.

3. The gander is weeping, *(three times)*
   Because his wife is dead.

4. The goslings are crying, *(three times)*
   Because their mama's dead.

5. She died in the water, *(three times)*
   With her heels above her head.

HAPPY TRAILS
from the Television Series THE ROY ROGERS SHOW

Words and Music by
DALE EVANS

HOME ON THE RANGE

Traditional

1. Oh, give me a home where the
2. of - ten at night where when the
3.,4. *See additional lyrics*

buf - fa - lo roam, where the deer and the
heav - ens are bright, where from the deer light and of the

an - te - lope play,_____ where
glit - ter - ing stars,_____ have I

Additional Lyrics

3. Where the air is so pure and the zephyrs so free,
   And the breezes so balmy and light;
   Oh, I would not exchange my home on the range
   For the glittering cities so bright.
   To Chorus

4. Oh, give me a land where the bright diamond sand
   Flows leisurely down with the stream,
   Where the graceful white swan glides slowly along,
   Like a maid in a heavenly dream.
   To Chorus

HEART AND SOUL
from the Paramount Short Subject A SONG IS BORN

Words by FRANK LOESSER
Music by HOAGY CARMICHAEL

HEIGH-HO

the Dwarfs' Marching Song from SNOW WHITE AND THE SEVEN DWARFS

Words by LARRY MOREY
Music by FRANK CHURCHILL

HI-DIDDLE-DEE-DEE
(AN ACTOR'S LIFE FOR ME)
from Walt Disney's PINOCCHIO

Words by NED WASHINGTON
Music by LEIGH HARLINE

The grass is al-ways green-er in the oth-er fel-low's

yard.___ No mat-ter what your life may be you think your life is

hard___ If we could pick and choose___ and na-ture was-n't a

HOUSE AT POOH CORNER

Words and Music by
KENNY LOGGINS

MCA music publishing

I LOVE TRASH

from the Television Series SESAME STREET

Words and Music by
JEFF MOSS

I DON'T WANT TO
LIVE ON THE MOON

from the Television Series SESAME STREET

Words and Music by
JEFF MOSS

I'M POPEYE THE SAILOR MAN

Theme from the Paramount Cartoon POPEYE THE SAILOR

Words and Music by
SAMMY LERNER

KUM BA YAH

Traditional

I'VE GOT NO STRINGS

from Walt Disney's PINOCCHIO

Words by NED WASHINGTON
Music by LEIGH HARLINE

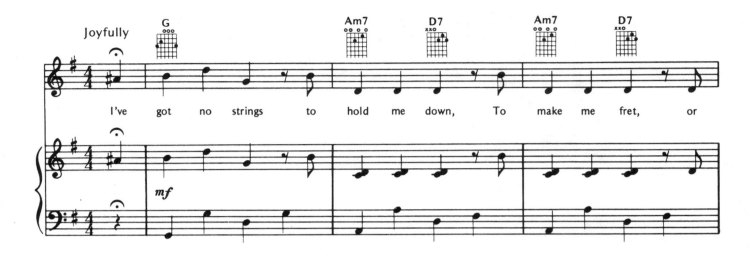

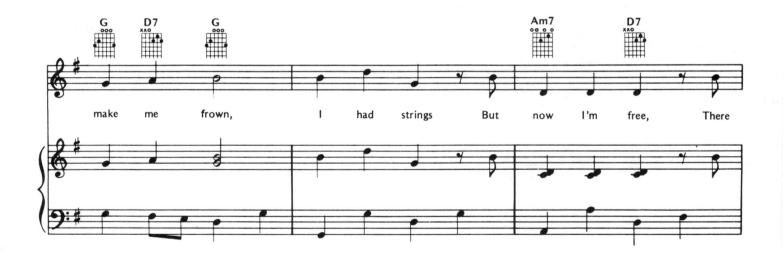

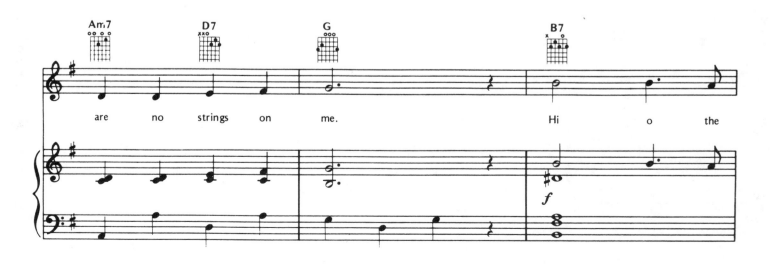

IT'S RAINING, IT'S POURING

Traditional

JESUS LOVES ME

Words by ANNA WARNER
Music by WILLIAM BRADBURY

LAZY MARY, WILL YOU GET UP?

Traditional

La-zy Mary, will you get up, will you get up, will
Oh, no, Moth-er, I won't get up, I won't get up, I

you get up? La-zy Ma-ry, will you get up? Will
won't get up. Oh, no, Moth-er, I won't get up, I

you get up to-day? _____
won't get up to- day. _____

MAGIC PENNY

Words and Music by
MALVINA REYNOLDS

LET'S GO FLY A KITE

from Walt Disney's MARY POPPINS

Words and Music by RICHARD M. SHERMAN
and ROBERT B. SHERMAN

LI'L LIZA JANE

Words and Music by
COUNTESS ADA de LACHAU

Additional Lyrics

3. I wouldn't care how far we roam, Li'l Liza Jane,
   Where she's at is home sweet home, Li'l Liza Jane.
   Oh, Eliza, Li'l Liza Jane!
   Oh, Eliza, Li'l Liza Jane

THE MARVELOUS TOY

Words and Music by
TOM PAXTON

Moderate tempo

When I was just a wee lit-tle lad full of health and
(The) first time that I picked it up I had a big sur-
(It) first marched left and then marched right and then marched un-der a
(Well the) years have gone by too quick-ly it seems and I have my own lit-tle

joy, My fa-ther home-ward came one night, and
prise, For right on its bot-tom were two big but-tons that
chair, And when I looked where it had gone, it
boy, And yes-ter-day I gave to him my

MY BONNIE LIES OVER THE OCEAN

Traditional

MARY HAD A LITTLE LAMB

Words by SARAH JOSEPHA HALE
Music is Traditional

MICHAEL
(ROW THE BOAT ASHORE)

Traditional Folksong

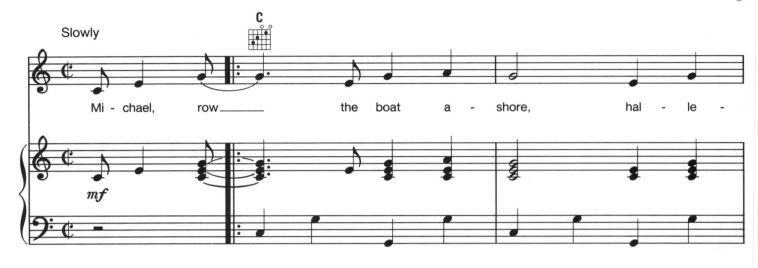

Slowly

Mi - chael, row_____ the boat a - shore, hal - le -

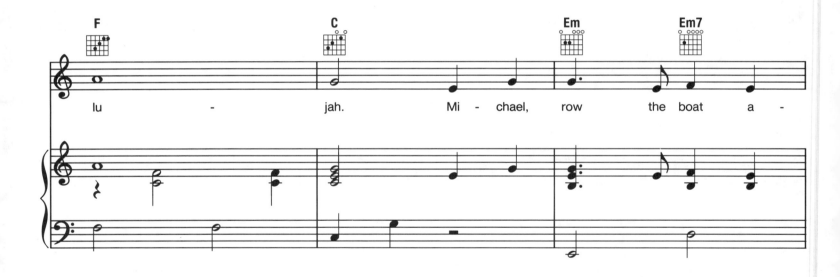

lu - jah. Mi - chael, row the boat a -

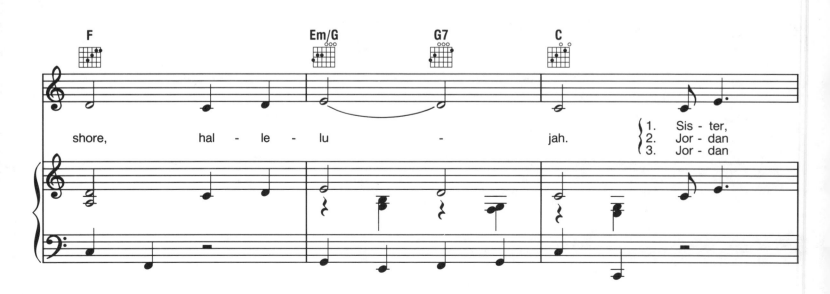

shore, hal - le - lu - jah.

1. Sis - ter,
2. Jor - dan
3. Jor - dan

THE MUFFIN MAN

Traditional

ON THE GOOD SHIP LOLLIPOP

from BRIGHT EYES

Words and Music by SIDNEY CLARE
and RICHARD A. WHITING

Lyrics:

On the good ship __ lol-li-pop, __ It's a sweet trip __ to a

can-dy shop, __ Where bon-bons play _____ on the sun-ny beach of

pep-per-mint bay. _____ Lem-on-ade stands __

OVER THE RIVER
AND THROUGH THE WOODS

Traditional

Lyrics:

O-ver the riv-er and through the woods, To grand-fa-ther's house we go;_____ The
O-ver the riv-er and through the woods, Oh, how__ the wind does blow!_____ It

horse knows the way to car-ry the sleigh thro' the white and drift-ed snow._____

stings the toes and bites the nose As o-ver the ground we go._____

THE PAW PAW PATCH

Traditional

RUBBER DUCKIE
from the Television Series SESAME STREET

Words and Music by
JEFF MOSS

PEOPLE IN YOUR NEIGHBORHOOD

from the Television Series SESAME STREET

Words and Music by
JEFF MOSS

PUFF THE MAGIC DRAGON

Words by LEONARD LIPTON
Music by PETER YARROW

* 3rd time, play verse twice
before proceeding to Chorus.

Additional Lyrics

2. Together they would travel on a boat with billowed sail.
   Jackie kept a lookout perched on Puff's gigantic tail.
   Noble kings and princes would bow whene'er they came.
   Pirate ships would low'r their flag when Puff roared out his name. **Oh!** *(To Chorus)*

3. A dragon lives forever, but not so little boys.
   Painted wings and giant rings make way for other toys.
   One gray night it happened, Jackie Paper came no more,
   And Puff that mighty dragon, he ceased his fearless roar.

4. His head was bent in sorrow, green tears fell like rain.
   Puff no longer went to play along the Cherry Lane.
   Without his lifelong friend, Puff could not be brave,
   So Puff that mighty dragon sadly slipped into his cave. **Oh!** *(To Chorus)*

* THE RETURN OF PUFF

5. Puff the Magic Dragon danced down the Cherry Lane.
   He came upon a little girl, Julie Maple was her name.
   She'd heard that Puff had gone away, but that can never be,
   So together they went sailing to the land called Honalee. *(To Chorus)*

SAILING, SAILING

Words and Music by
GODFREY MARKS

SING
from SESAME STREET

Words and Music by
JOE RAPOSO

SING A SONG OF SIXPENCE

Traditional

A SPOONFUL OF SUGAR

from Walt Disney's MARY POPPINS

Words and Music by RICHARD M. SHERMAN
and ROBERT B. SHERMAN

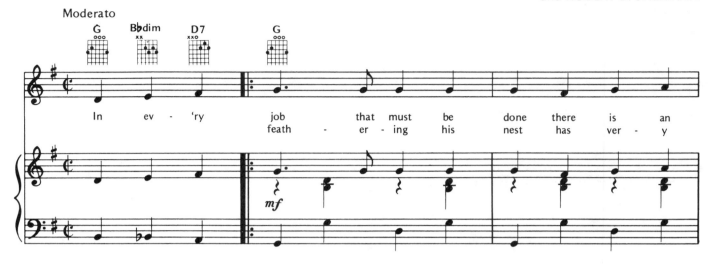

In ev-'ry job that must be done there is an
feath-er-ing his done nest has ver-y

el-e-ment of fun; You find the fun and
lit-tle time to rest While gath-er-ing his

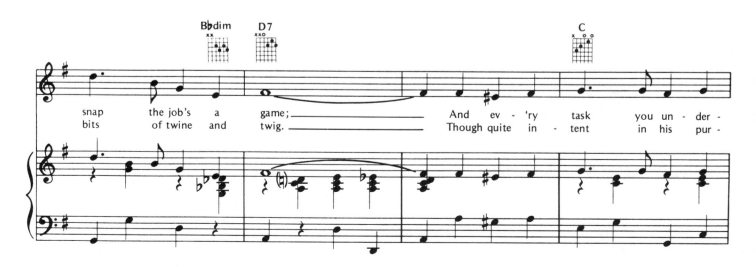

snap the job's a game;_____ And ev-'ry task you un-der-
bits of twine and twig._____ Though quite in-tent in his pur-

take he has a be - comes a piece of cake, A lark! A
suit he has a mer - ry tune to toot; He knows a

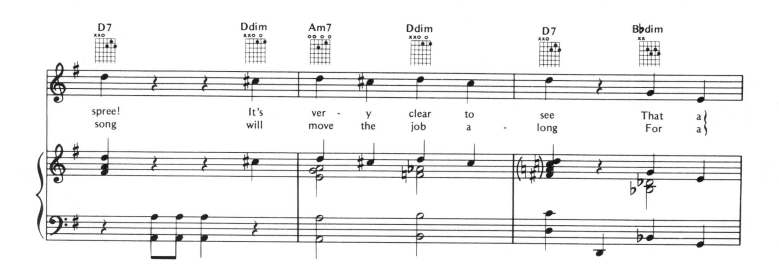

spree! It's ver - y clear to see That a
song will move the job a - long For a

spoon - ful of su - gar helps the med - i - cine go

TAKE ME OUT TO THE BALL GAME

Words by JACK NORWORTH
Music by ALBERT von TILZER

Take me out to the ball game

Take me out to the crowd. _____

SWEET BETSY FROM PIKE

Traditional

one spot-ted hog, say-ing good-bye, Pike Coun-ty, fare-well for a-while. We'll _

come back a-gain when we've panned out our pile. (2.-8.) panned out our pile.

Additional Lyrics

2. One evening quite early they camped on the Platte,
   'Twas near by the road on a green shady flat,
   Where Betsy, sore-footed, lay down to repose —
   With wonder Ike gazed on that Pike County rose.
   To Chorus

3. Their wagon broke down with a terrible crash,
   And out on the prairie rolled all kinds of trash,
   A few little baby clothes done up with care,
   'Twas rather suspicious, but all on the square.
   To Chorus

4. The Shanghai ran off, and their cattle all died;
   That morning the last piece of bacon was fried;
   Poor Ike was discouraged and Betsy got mad,
   The dog drooped his tail and looked wondrously sad.
   To Chorus

5. They soon reached the desert where Betsy gave out,
   And down in the sand she lay rolling about;
   While Ike, half distracted, looked on with surprise,
   Saying, "Betsy, get up, you'll get sand in your eyes."
   To Chorus

6. Sweet Betsy got up in a great deal of pain,
   Declared she'd go back to Pike County again;
   But Ike gave a sigh, and they fondly embraced,
   And they travelled along with his arm 'round her waist.
   To Chorus

7. They suddenly stopped on a very high hill,
   With wonder looked down upon old Placerville;
   Ike sighed when he said, and he cast his eyes down,
   "Sweet Betsy, my darling, we've got to Hangtown."
   To Chorus

8. Long Ike and sweet Betsy attended a dance;
   Ike wore a pair of his Pike County pants;
   Sweet Betsy was dressed up in ribbons and rings;
   Says Ike, "You're an angel, but where are your wings?"
   To Chorus

THERE'S A HOLE IN THE BUCKET

Traditional

Additional Lyrics

3. With what shall I fix it, dear Liza, etc.
4. With a straw, dear Henry, etc.
5. But the straw is too long, dear Liza, etc.
6. Then cut it, dear Henry, etc.
7. With what shall I cut it, dear Liza, etc.
8. With a knife, dear Henry, etc.
9. But the knife is too dull, dear Liza, etc.
10. Then sharpen it, dear Liza, etc.

11. With what shall I sharpen it, dear Liza, etc.
12. With a stone, dear Henry, etc.
13. But the stone is too dry, dear Liza, etc.
14. Then wet it, dear Henry, etc.
15. With what shall I wet it, dear Liza, etc.
16. With water, dear Henry, etc.
17. In what shall I carry it, dear Liza, etc.
18. In a bucket, dear Henry, etc.

19. There's a hole in the bucket, dear Liza, etc.

THE UNBIRTHDAY SONG

from Walt Disney's ALICE IN WONDERLAND

Words and Music by MACK DAVID,
AL HOFFMAN and JERRY LIVINGSTON

Refrain

Patter

THERE'S A HOLE IN THE BOTTOM OF THE SEA

Traditional

bump on the log in the hole in the bot-tom of the sea.

E

Faster still

C7 F

There's a frog on the bump on the log in the hole in the

C7

bot-tom of the sea, there's a frog on the bump on the

F

log in the hole in the bot-tom of the sea.

THIS TRAIN

Traditional

With spirit

1. This train is bound for glo - ry, this train. ___
2.-6. *See additional lyrics*

This train is bound for glo - ry,

this train. ___ This train is

Additional Lyrics

2. This train don't carry no gamblers, (*3 times*)
   No hypocrites, no midnight ramblers,
   This train is bound for glory, this train.

3. This train don't carry no liars, (*3 times*)
   No hypocrites and no high flyers,
   This train is bound for glory, this train.

4. This train is built for speed now, (*3 times*)
   Fastest train you ever did see,
   This train is bound for glory, this train.

5. This train you don't pay no transportation, (*3 times*)
   No Jim Crow and no discrimination,
   This train is bound for glory, this train.

6. This train don't carry no rustlers, (*3 times*)
   Sidestreet walkers, two-bit hustlers,
   This train is bound for glory, this train.

UNDER THE SEA
from Walt Disney's THE LITTLE MERMAID

Lyrics by HOWARD ASHMAN
Music by ALAN MENKEN

Just look ___ at the world a - round you, right here ___ on the
But fish ___ in the bowl is luck - y, they in ___ for a

o - cean floor. Such won - der - ful things sur - round you.
wors - er fate. One day ___ when the boss get hun - gry

What more ___ is you look - in' for?
guess who ___ gon' be on the plate. } Un - der the

sea, un - der the sea.

WHEN JOHNNY COMES MARCHING HOME

Words and Music by
PATRICK SARSFIELD GILMORE (LOUIS LAMBERT)

Moving along, in 2

When John-ny comes march-ing home a-gain, Hur-rah! _____ Hur-rah! _____ we'll give him a heart-y wel-come then, Hur-

WHEN THE SAINTS GO MARCHING IN

Words by KATHERINE E. PURVIS
Music by JAMES M. BLACK

WHO'S AFRAID OF THE BIG BAD WOLF?

from Walt Disney's THREE LITTLE PIGS

Words and Music by FRANK CHURCHILL
Additional Lyric by ANN RONELL

Who's a-fraid of the big bad wolf, big bad wolf, big bad wolf?

Who's a-fraid of the big bad wolf Tra-la-la-la-la. la. Long a-

go there were three pigs, lit-tle hand-some pig-gy-wigs, For the big bad, ver-y big

WON'T YOU BE MY NEIGHBOR?
(a/k/a IT'S A BEAUTIFUL DAY IN THIS NEIGHBORHOOD)
from MISTER ROGERS' NEIGHBORHOOD

Words and Music by
FRED ROGERS

ZIP-A-DEE-DOO-DAH
from Walt Disney's SONG OF THE SOUTH

Words by RAY GILBERT
Music by ALLIE WRUBEL

A WHOLE NEW WORLD

from Walt Disney's ALADDIN

Music by ALAN MENKEN
Lyrics by TIM RICE